40 Minute
BIBLE STUDIES

6-WEEK
STUDY PROGRAM

BUILDING A

MARRIAGE

THAT REALLY

WORKS

PRECEPT
MINISTRIES
INTERNATIONAL

KAY ARTHUR
DAVID & BJ LAWSON

BUILDING A MARRIAGE THAT REALLY WORKS
PUBLISHED BY WATERBROOK PRESS
2375 Telstar Drive, Suite 160
Colorado Springs, Colorado 80920
A division of Random House, Inc.

All Scripture quotations, unless otherwise indicated, are taken from the *New American Standard Bible®* (NASB). © Copyright The Lockman Foundation 1960, 1962, 1963, 1968, 1971, 1972, 1973, 1975, 1977, 1995. Used by permission. (www.Lockman.org).

Italics in Scripture quotations reflect the author's added emphasis.

ISBN 1-57856-909-5

Printed in the United States of America
2004—First Edition

10 9 8 7 6 5 4 3 2 1

HOW TO USE THIS STUDY

This small-group study is for people who are interested in learning for themselves more about what the Bible says on various subjects, but who have only limited time to meet together. It's ideal, for example, for a lunch group at work, an early morning men's group, a young mothers' group meeting in a home, a Sunday-school class, or even family devotions. (It's also ideal for small groups that typically have longer meeting times—such as evening groups or Saturday morning groups—but want to devote only a portion of their time together to actual study, while reserving the rest for prayer, fellowship, or other activities.)

This book is designed so that all the group's participants will complete each lesson's study activities *at the same time.* Discussing your insights drawn from what God says about the subject reveals exciting, life-impacting truths.

Although it's a group study, you'll need a facilitator to lead the study and keep the discussion moving. (This person's function is *not* that of a lecturer or teacher. However, when this book is used in a Sunday-school class or similar setting, the teacher should feel free to lead more directly and to bring in other insights in addition to those provided in each week's lesson.)

If *you* are your group's facilitator, the leader, here are some helpful points for making your job easier:

- Go through the lesson and mark the text before you lead the group. This will give you increased familiarity with the material and will enable you to facilitate the group with greater ease. It may be easier for you to lead the group through the instructions for marking if you, as a leader, choose a specific color for each symbol you mark.

- As you lead the group, start at the beginning of the text and simply read it aloud in the order it appears in the lesson, including the "insight boxes," which appear throughout. Work through the lesson together, observing and discussing what you learn. As you read the Scripture verses, have the group say aloud the word they are marking in the text.

- The discussion questions are there simply to help you cover the material. As the class moves into the discussion, many times you will find that they will cover the questions on their own. Remember, the discussion questions are there to guide the group through the topic, not to squelch discussion.

- Remember how important it is for people to verbalize their answers and discoveries. This greatly strengthens their personal understanding of each week's lesson. Try to ensure that everyone has plenty of opportunity to contribute to each week's discussions.

- Keep the discussion moving. This may mean spending more time on some parts of the study than on others. If necessary, you should feel free to spread out a lesson over more than one session. However, remember that you don't want to slow the pace too much. It's much better to leave everyone "wanting more" than to have people dropping out because of declining interest.

- If the validity or accuracy of some of the answers seems questionable, you can gently and cheerfully remind the group to stay focused on the truth of the Scriptures. Your object is to learn what the Bible says, not to engage in human philosophy. Simply stick with the Scriptures and give God the opportunity to speak. His Word *is* truth (John 17:17)!

BUILDING A MARRIAGE THAT REALLY WORKS

As children, little girls often used to play dress up, with a blanket draped over their heads to serve as a "bride's veil" as they dreamed about their future wedding day. Together, little girls and boys played "house," with Daddy going to work and Mommy taking care of the kids and cooking the meals. Daddy would come home and kiss Mommy, then they would sit down to dinner and talk about the events of the day.

Such innocent days soon gave way to grownup responsibilities, where the experience of real-life marriage seems much more difficult than we dreamed as children. And in these days where the definitions of family and home have been stretched and challenged, the husband-wife relationship presents more challenges than ever before. Divorce has either directly or indirectly affected virtually all of us. Blended families and multiple-income households seem to be the standard of our day.

So how can we follow God's design for marriage in our modern-day world? In the weeks ahead we will take a look at the institution of marriage and the roles of the husband and the wife, as well as examine key principles regarding communication, love, and finances. Through this study you will discover how to establish and maintain the kind of marriage God intended you to have—one that will last "until death us do part."

After God created the heavens and the earth and everything on the earth, He formed the most magnificent of all His creatures—man and woman. More detail is given regarding the sixth day of creation than any of the others, indicating the significance of these distinctive creations. God created man and woman for a unique relationship with Him and with each other.

We are going to begin our study this week by looking at God's design for marriage. Can it truly be a permanent, meaningful, joyful relationship?

OBSERVE

Genesis is the book of beginnings. Let's take a look at the Creation account of man and woman and the beginning of this institution we call "marriage."

Leader: Read aloud Genesis 1:26-28.
  • *Have the group underline every reference to **man**, including any pronouns.*

DISCUSS

• What did you learn from marking *man* in each verse?

• What did you learn from these verses about male and female?

GENESIS 1:26-28

26 Then God said, "Let Us make man in Our image, according to Our likeness; and let them rule over the fish of the sea and over the birds of the sky and over the cattle and over all the earth, and over every creeping thing that creeps on the earth."

27 God created man in His own image, in the image of God He created him; male and female He created them.

28 God blessed them; and God said to them, "Be fruitful and multiply, and fill the earth, and subdue it; and rule over the fish of the sea and over the birds of the sky and over every living thing that moves on the earth."

• What role and responsibilities did God give to both male and female in verse 28?

• Could God's instructions be carried out by two men or two women? What does this tell you about the institution of marriage?

• Discuss why it is significant that God gave the same responsibilities to both the male and the female.

INSIGHT

Genesis 1 gives us the big picture of Creation, an overview that tells us at a glance what happened from the first day of Creation through the sixth. In Genesis 2, God focuses on the details of man's creation. Some consider the two accounts in chapters 1 and 2 contradictory, but they are not. They simply record the events from different perspectives.

OBSERVE

The beginning of Genesis 2 gives us further insight into man's creation.

Leader: Read aloud Genesis 2:7-8,18-20. Have the group…

> • *mark every reference to **God,** including pronouns, with a triangle:* △
>
> • *underline every reference to **man,** including pronouns and synonyms.*

DISCUSS

• What did you learn from marking the references to man?

• After God created man and placed him in the garden, what did God say?

• According to these verses, why did God make woman?

GENESIS 2:7-8,18-20

7 Then the LORD God formed man of dust from the ground, and breathed into his nostrils the breath of life; and man became a living being.

8 The LORD God planted a garden toward the east, in Eden; and there He placed the man whom He had formed.

18 Then the LORD God said, "It is not good for the man to be alone; I will make him a helper suitable for him."

19 Out of the ground the LORD God formed every beast of the field and every bird of the sky, and brought them to the man to see what

he would call them; and whatever the man called a living creature, that was its name.

20 The man gave names to all the cattle, and to the birds of the sky, and to every beast of the field, but for Adam there was not found a helper suitable for him.

INSIGHT

Man needed "a helper suitable for him." The word for *helper* in Hebrew does not mean "servant" or "slave." The word is most commonly used in the Bible in reference to God as our helper, often in a military sense. A helper in this sense would be some-one—superior or equal—who comes alongside to support another in a situation that can't be handled alone. According to this passage, man needed help—a partner every bit his equal whose strengths would compensate for his weaknesses.

GENESIS 2:21-24

21 So the LORD God caused a deep sleep to fall upon the man, and he slept; then He took one of his ribs and closed up the flesh at that place.

22 The LORD God fashioned into a

OBSERVE

Leader: *Read aloud Genesis 2:21-24.*

• *Have the group circle every reference to* **woman,** *including pronouns.*

DISCUSS

• Discuss how God created the woman.

• Looking at what you've marked in this passage, ask the "5 Ws and an H"—who, what, when, where, why, and how—to see what the text tells you about woman.

• **Why** was she created?

• **When** was she created, relative to man's creation?

• For **whom** was she created? Why was this important?

• According to verse 23, **what** did man say when God brought the woman to him?

• "For this reason" in verse 24 refers back to verses 21-23. According to verse 24, what is to happen when a couple marries?

woman the rib which He had taken from the man, and brought her to the man.

23 The man said, "This is now bone of my bones, and flesh of my flesh; she shall be called Woman, because she was taken out of Man."

24 For this reason a man shall leave his father and his mother, and be joined to his wife; and they shall become one flesh.

INSIGHT

The term "joined to" (translated "cleave" in some Bibles) means "to glue together, to adhere to, to stick to." It carries the idea of loyalty and devotion.

Imagine two pieces of construction paper, one red and one green. If you were to glue them together and let the glue dry, what would happen if you pulled them apart? Would there be a clean break? No, you would find that some of the red still clings or adheres to the green and vice versa. You could expect some tearing as well.

The same is true of a marriage relationship. Once two people are joined together in marriage, there's no such thing as a "clean break" when it comes to divorce. Even if no children are involved, the participants will experience a tearing of intimacy, emotions, etc.

• What does the phrase "one flesh" tell us about God's plan for marriage?

• When two become "one" in marriage, they are joined together. What happens if they separate from one another?

• Discuss how knowing this should affect the marriage relationship.

OBSERVE

Leader: Read 1 Corinthians 6:15-16 aloud.

• *Have the group draw a box around every reference to* **bodies** *or* **members,** *including pronouns.*

DISCUSS

• What did you learn from this passage about the sexual relationship?

1 CORINTHIANS 6:15-16

15 Do you not know that your bodies are members of Christ? Shall I then take away the members of Christ and make them members of a prostitute? May it never be!

16 Or do you not know that the one who joins himself to a prostitute is one body with her? For He says, "The two shall become one flesh."

MATTHEW 19:3-10

3 Some Pharisees came to Jesus, testing Him and asking, "Is it lawful for a man to divorce his wife for any reason at all?"

4 And He answered and said, "Have you not read that He who created them from the beginning made them male and female,

5 and said, 'For this reason a man shall leave his father and mother and be joined to his wife, and the two shall become one flesh'?

6 "So they are no longer two, but one flesh. What therefore God has joined together, let no man separate."

OBSERVE

So far we have seen that God intended marriage to be permanent. Are there any exceptions to this?

Leader: Read Matthew 19:3-10 aloud. Have the group say aloud and mark...

- *every reference to **God**, including pronouns, with a triangle:* △
- *every reference to **divorce**, including pronouns, with a slash, like this:* /

DISCUSS

- What do you discern to be God's attitude toward marriage? Why?

- Why did Moses permit divorce, according to these verses?

- What does the desire to divorce one's mate reveal about the condition of the heart?

• According to verse 9, if a person divorces his or her mate and marries another, what is he or she guilty of?

7 They said to Him, "Why then did Moses command to give her a certificate of divorce and send her away?"

• What are the exceptions, if any, to this?

8 He said to them, "Because of your hardness of heart Moses permitted you to divorce your wives; but from the beginning it has not been this way.

• Why do you suppose this is true?

9 "And I say to you, whoever divorces his wife, except for immorality, and marries another woman commits adultery."

• What conclusion did the disciples draw from this teaching?

10 The disciples said to Him, "If the relationship of the man with his wife is like this, it is better not to marry."

• How does knowing this affect your attitude about marriage?

MALACHI 2:13-16

13 "This is another thing you do: you cover the altar of the LORD with tears, with weeping and with groaning, because He no longer regards the offering or accepts it with favor from your hand.

14 "Yet you say, 'For what reason?' Because the LORD has been a witness between you and the wife of your youth, against whom you have dealt treacherously, though she is your companion and your wife by covenant.

15 "But not one has done so who has a remnant of the Spirit. And what did that one do while he was seeking a godly offspring?

OBSERVE

Let's look at an Old Testament passage that touches on God's view of divorce.

Leader: Read Malachi 2:13-16 aloud. Have the group...
- *circle every reference to **wife**, including pronouns.*
- *mark **divorce** with a slash, as before.*

DISCUSS

• Why wouldn't God accept the offering the people were bringing?

• How did the people respond to His rejection of their offerings?

• What did you learn by marking *divorce*?

OBSERVE

Before we wrap up this week's study, let's examine one other verse that describes God's perspective on marriage.

Leader: *Read aloud Hebrews 13:4.*
   • *Have the group draw a box around each occurrence of* **marriage.**

DISCUSS

• According to this verse, how is marriage to be regarded?

• What would defile the marriage bed?

• What will God do to those who defile it?

• Summarize and discuss what you've learned about marriage this week.

Take heed then to your spirit, and let no one deal treacherously against the wife of your youth.

16 "For I hate divorce," says the LORD, the God of Israel, "and him who covers his garment with wrong," says the LORD of hosts. "So take heed to your spirit, that you do not deal treacherously."

HEBREWS 13:4

Marriage is to be held in honor among all, and the marriage bed is to be undefiled; for fornicators and adulterers God will judge.

WRAP IT UP

God designed Adam and Eve for a unique relationship with Him. No other creatures enjoyed this kind of union. The first couple was made in God's image, was given dominion over the rest of creation, and enjoyed daily fellowship with the Creator.

Tragically, Adam and Eve made a wrong choice; they ate the forbidden fruit and sin entered the world. In the weeks ahead, we'll look at how this affected the marriage relationship. For now, we need to acknowledge that, because of sin, marriage takes work; however, God enables believers to succeed despite the challenges by providing not only an instruction manual but also His Holy Spirit, who enables us to carry out the instructions in Scripture. All we have to do is to follow the directions carefully.

God intended marriage to be permanent, an intimate relationship in which two are irrevocably joined together as one. Marriage is an earthly picture of the relationship between Jesus and His church, the bride of Christ. Marriages are intended to be living testimonies of Jesus' inseparable union with believers. When husbands and wives fight, grow distant, or separate, God's portrait of the spiritual relationship is marred. We'll learn more about this in upcoming lessons.

Our society puts pressure on men to succeed in the realms of work and physical competition, while downplaying the importance of their relationships. Many men tend to throw themselves into their work until it consumes their lives. At night, the average husband comes home exhausted, ready to shut down and zone out emotionally and mentally. Often he abandons his family emotionally, physically, spiritually, and sometimes even financially. Other men take the opposite path, finding reasons to avoid work while ignoring their family responsibilities.

This week we will see what God has to say about the role of the husband in marriage. Is work and providing for his family his only responsibility? Is he free to do as he pleases with his own time, independent of his family's needs or desires? Let's look to Scripture for the answers to these questions.

OBSERVE

As we begin our study, let's review the responsibilities God placed on the man and the woman just after He created them.

Leader: Read Genesis 2:8-9,15-25.

- *Underline every reference to **man**, including pronouns.*

GENESIS 2:8-9,15-25

8 The LORD God planted a garden toward the east, in Eden; and there He placed the man whom He had formed.

9 Out of the ground the LORD God caused to grow every tree that is pleasing to the sight and good for food; the tree of life also in the midst

of the garden, and the tree of the knowledge of good and evil.

15 Then the LORD God took the man and put him into the garden of Eden to cultivate it and keep it.

16 The LORD God commanded the man, saying, "From any tree of the garden you may eat freely;

17 but from the tree of the knowledge of good and evil you shall not eat, for in the day that you eat from it you will surely die."

18 Then the LORD God said, "It is not good for the man to be alone; I will make him a helper suitable for him."

19 Out of the ground the LORD God formed

DISCUSS

• Discuss what you learned from these passages about man.

• What was God's plan for man in the area of work? in the area of relationship? Explain your answers.

every beast of the field and every bird of the sky, and brought them to the man to see what he would call them; and whatever the man called a living creature, that was its name.

20 The man gave names to all the cattle, and to the birds of the sky, and to every beast of the field, but for Adam there was not found a helper suitable for him.

21 So the LORD God caused a deep sleep to fall upon the man, and he slept; then He took one of his ribs and closed up the flesh at that place.

22 The LORD God fashioned into a woman the rib which He had taken from the man, and brought her to the man.

23 The man said, "This is now bone of my bones, and flesh of my flesh; she shall be called Woman, because she was taken out of Man."

24 For this reason a man shall leave his father and his mother, and be joined to his wife; and they shall become one flesh.

25 And the man and his wife were both naked and were not ashamed.

1 CORINTHIANS 11:3,8-12

3 But I want you to understand that Christ is the head of every man, and the man is the head of a woman, and God is the head of Christ.

8 For man does not originate from woman, but woman from man;

OBSERVE

Leader: *Read aloud 1 Corinthians 11:3, 8-12. Have the group...*
- *underline every reference to **man**.*
- *circle every reference to **woman**.*

DISCUSS

• What did you learn from 1 Corinthians about the relationship between the man and the woman?

• From what you have studied, does God intend for the woman to be considered inferior to the man in status? Explain your answer.

OBSERVE

Leader: *Read Galatians 3:28 aloud. Have the group…*

> • *underline the word **male**.*
> • *circle the word **female**.*

DISCUSS

• What light does this verse shed on the passage from 1 Corinthians?

9 for indeed man was not created for the woman's sake, but woman for the man's sake.

10 Therefore the woman ought to have a symbol of authority on her head, because of the angels.

11 However, in the Lord, neither is woman independent of man, nor is man independent of woman.

12 For as the woman originates from the man, so also the man has his birth through the woman; and all things originate from God.

GALATIANS 3:28

There is neither Jew nor Greek, there is neither slave nor free man, there is neither male nor female; for you are all one in Christ Jesus.

GENESIS 3:1-13,16-24

1 Now the serpent was more crafty than any beast of the field which the LORD God had made. And he said to the woman, "Indeed, has God said, 'You shall not eat from any tree of the garden'?"

2 The woman said to the serpent, "From the fruit of the trees of the garden we may eat;

3 but from the fruit of the tree which is in the middle of the garden, God has said, 'You shall not eat from it or touch it, or you will die.'"

4 The serpent said to the woman, "You surely will not die!

5 "For God knows that in the day you eat

OBSERVE

Leader: Read Genesis 3:1-13,16-24 aloud. Have the group...

- underline every reference to **man,** including pronouns.
- circle every reference to **woman,** including pronouns.

DISCUSS

- Discuss what you learned from marking *man* and *woman.*

- Who first ate of the fruit of the tree?

• What happened when they ate the fruit?

• When God questioned Adam about what he and Eve had done, what was Adam's response?

from it your eyes will be opened, and you will be like God, knowing good and evil."

6 When the woman saw that the tree was good for food, and that it was a delight to the eyes, and that the tree was desirable to make one wise, she took from its fruit and ate; and she gave also to her husband with her, and he ate.

7 Then the eyes of both of them were opened, and they knew that they were naked; and they sewed fig leaves together and made themselves loin coverings.

8 They heard the sound of the LORD God walking in the garden in the cool of the day, and the man and his wife hid

themselves from the presence of the LORD God among the trees of the garden.

9 Then the LORD God called to the man, and said to him, "Where are you?"

10 He said, "I heard the sound of You in the garden, and I was afraid because I was naked; so I hid myself."

11 And He said, "Who told you that you were naked? Have you eaten from the tree of which I commanded you not to eat?"

12 The man said, "The woman whom You gave to be with me, she gave me from the tree, and I ate."

13 Then the LORD God said to the woman, "What is this you have

• What can you learn from Adam's response and from God's that could pertain to your own marriage?

• When God questioned Eve about what she did, what was her response?

• What did God say would be Adam's position in respect to Eve after the Fall? Note the verse.

• What consequence(s) did Adam receive for his actions?

done?" And the woman said, "The serpent deceived me, and I ate."

16 To the woman He said, "I will greatly multiply your pain in childbirth, in pain you will bring forth children; yet your desire will be for your husband, and he will rule over you."

17 Then to Adam He said, "Because you have listened to the voice of your wife, and have eaten from the tree about which I commanded you, saying, 'You shall not eat from it'; cursed is the ground because of you; in toil you will eat of it all the days of your life.

18 "Both thorns and thistles it shall grow for you; and you will eat the plants of the field;

19 By the sweat of your face you will eat bread, till you return to the ground, because from it you were taken; for you are dust, and to dust you shall return."

20 Now the man called his wife's name Eve, because she was the mother of all the living.

21 The LORD God made garments of skin for Adam and his wife, and clothed them.

22 Then the LORD God said, "Behold, the man has become like one of Us, knowing good and evil; and now, he might stretch out his hand, and take also from the tree of life, and eat, and live forever"—

• From all you have read so far, what seems to be the man's primary role from verse 16 on? Why?

• What did you learn from the responses of Adam and Eve that could apply to marriage?

• Discuss the responsibilities God placed on Adam as a result of the Fall and how they compare to his responsibilities prior to the Fall.

OBSERVE

We saw from the previous passage that the ground was cursed for man's sake, because of his sin. His work would now occupy a great deal of time, as God made man responsible to provide for his family. Most men do this well; however, more and more we hear about "deadbeat dads" who don't assume responsibility for their children or men who waste their income on frivolous pleasures while their families are in need. Let's see what God says about this.

Leader: Read the following passages: Exodus 34:21; 2 Thessalonians 3:6-12; and 1 Timothy 5:8. Have the group…
- *draw a rectangle around every reference to **work,** including synonyms like **provide**.*
- *underline each occurrence of the words **unruly** and **undisciplined**.*

DISCUSS

- Discuss what you learned from these passages about the responsibility of man as provider for his family.

23 therefore the LORD God sent him out from the garden of Eden, to cultivate the ground from which he was taken.

24 So He drove the man out; and at the east of the garden of Eden He stationed the cherubim and the flaming sword which turned every direction to guard the way to the tree of life.

EXODUS 34:21

You shall work six days, but on the seventh day you shall rest; even during plowing time and harvest you shall rest.

2 THESSALONIANS 3:6-12

6 Now we command you, brethren, in the name of our Lord Jesus Christ, that you keep away from every brother who leads an unruly life and not according to the tradition which you received from us.

⁷ For you yourselves know how you ought to follow our example, because we did not act in an undisciplined manner among you,

⁸ nor did we eat anyone's bread without paying for it, but with labor and hardship we kept working night and day so that we would not be a burden to any of you;

⁹ not because we do not have the right to this, but in order to offer ourselves as a model for you, so that you would follow our example.

• What did you learn from marking references to work and being undisciplined?

• According to these passages, what responsibility does a man bear for his family, his household?

• If he fails to do as God expects, what should happen? How is such a man described in 1 Timothy 5:8?

10 For even when we were with you, we used to give you this order: if anyone is not willing to work, then he is not to eat, either.

11 For we hear that some among you are leading an undisciplined life, doing no work at all, but acting like busybodies.

12 Now such persons we command and exhort in the Lord Jesus Christ to work in quiet fashion and eat their own bread.

1 Timothy 5:8

But if anyone does not provide for his own, and especially for those of his household, he has denied the faith and is worse than an unbeliever.

1 Corinthians 11:3

But I want you to understand that Christ is the head of every man, and the man is the head of a woman, and God is the head of Christ.

OBSERVE

Let's turn now to another aspect of the man's role within a family.

Leader: Read 1 Corinthians 11:3 aloud. Have the group do the following:
- *Underline every reference to **man**.*
- *Circle each occurrence of **woman**.*

DISCUSS

- Draw a simple diagram that depicts the authority structure described in this verse.

- Who is the head of every man? To whom is man responsible to submit?

- If a man doesn't submit, what is he demonstrating to his wife?

- Whose responsibility is it to make a man submit? Is it the wife's responsibility to bring the husband under the authority of Christ?

OBSERVE

Leader: Read Ephesians 5:22-33 aloud. Have the group...

- *underline every reference to **husband(s)**, including pronouns and synonyms.*
- *draw a box around words and phrases like **as, but as,** and **just as** that alert us to a **comparison** within the text.*

EPHESIANS 5:22-33

22 Wives, be subject to your own husbands, as to the Lord.

23 For the husband is the head of the wife, as Christ also is the head of the church, He Himself being the Savior of the body.

24 But as the church is subject to Christ, so also the wives ought to be to their husbands in everything.

25 Husbands, love your wives, just as Christ also loved the church and gave Himself up for her,

26 so that He might sanctify her, having cleansed her by the washing of water with the word,

27 that He might present to Himself the church in all her glory, having no spot or wrinkle or any such thing; but that she would be holy and blameless.

28 So husbands ought also to love their own wives as their own bodies. He who loves his own wife loves himself;

29 for no one ever hated his own flesh, but nourishes and cherishes it, just as Christ also does the church,

30 because we are members of His body.

31 For this reason a man shall leave his father and mother and shall be joined to his wife, and the two shall become one flesh.

INSIGHT

Understanding the words *love, nourish,* and *cherish* is vital to grasping the unique role of the man in marriage.

The word translated here as *love* is the Greek word *agapao;* it denotes an unconditional love that desires the highest good of the one being loved. The present tense of the Greek verb indicates a continuous, habitual action. This type of love is not simply an emotion; it is also a choice.

The word *nourish* means "to nurture, rear, feed."

Cherish means "to heat, to soften by heat, to keep warm." It is used to describe birds covering their young with their feathers. It indicates the action of fostering with tender care and love. Again, the present tense in verse 29 denotes a continuous, habitual action.

DISCUSS

• What did you observe from marking the instructions to the husband?

• What example of love does Paul give in this passage?

INSIGHT

In this passage, God tells husbands to love their wives "as Christ also loved the church." A husband is to nourish and cherish his wife, not simply because she needs it but because he is to be a picture of Jesus Christ. A husband is to his wife as Christ is to His bride, the church. The husband is to be a living epistle, read by all men. By his character and lifestyle, a man either shows the character and work of Jesus Christ for His church or mars the portrait God intended marriage to present.

• To what degree is a man to love his wife?

32 This mystery is great; but I am speaking with reference to Christ and the church.

33 Nevertheless, each individual among you also is to love his own wife even as himself, and the wife must see to it that she respects her husband.

1 PETER 3:7

You husbands in the same way, live with your wives in an understanding way, as with someone weaker, since she is a woman; and show her honor as a fellow heir of the grace of life, so that your prayers will not be hindered.

COLOSSIANS 3:19

Husbands, love your wives and do not be embittered against them.

EPHESIANS 5:25

Husbands, love your wives, just as Christ also loved the church and gave Himself up for her.

OBSERVE

We've seen that the husband is to the wife as Christ is to the church. Because the man is to love his wife as Christ loved the church, and since he is also the head, headship must take place within the context of love. Let's look further at this aspect of a husband's role in marriage.

Leader: Read the following passages aloud: 1 Peter 3:7; Colossians 3:19; and Ephesians 5:25.

- *Have the group underline every reference to **husbands,** including pronouns.*

DISCUSS

- Discuss what you learned about the role of the husband from these verses.

- What will happen if a husband doesn't follow the instructions of 1 Peter 3:7?

• What reasons have you heard men give for abdicating their responsibilities as husbands and fathers?

• How does their thinking compare with what you have learned from our study this week?

• Name five things a husband can do to love, nourish, and cherish his wife.

WRAP IT UP

The verses we've read this week reveal that God holds husbands responsible to provide for their families and to love their wives. God's design for marriage involves a husband who loves his wife unconditionally, just as Christ loved the Church. He requires of husbands the same sort of self-giving, unconditional, sacrificial love that Jesus demonstrated when He laid down His life for sinful mankind. What a high calling and awesome responsibility!

Can you imagine what would happen if every husband made his wife and family his top priority, after God? The divorce rate would plummet. Homes would be restored. Children would find the security, peace, and joy their hearts crave.

Husband, are you a servant leader who illustrates Christ's love and headship or a dictator who barks out orders? How can you encourage your wife today? How can you show her the kind of love you've read about this week? How can you minister to her needs? Are you working? If not, why not? If so, are you working to the detriment of your wife and family? Have you focused so narrowly on your role of provider that you've failed in your responsibility to love?

Take some time now to identify at least one action you can take this week to more effectively fulfill your God-given role.

WEEK THREE

The traditional roles of men and women have been radically challenged and changed in the past few years. Women are told they can do it all and have it all. They're encouraged to be emotionally and financially independent of their husbands, and they feel pressured to juggle the responsibilities of the workplace and family simultaneously.

This week we are going to look at God's truths concerning the woman's role in marriage. Knowing these truths will keep you from being drawn into the web of the world's lies.

OBSERVE

Although we have already looked at the creation of man and woman in Genesis 1, let's return there once more for the purpose of looking at the role of the woman.

Leader: Read aloud Genesis 1:26-28; 2:18, 21-25. Have the group do the following:
- *Underline every reference to **man**, including pronouns and synonyms.*
- *Circle every reference to **woman**, including pronouns and synonyms.*
- *Double underline every occurrence of **them**.*

GENESIS 1:26-28

26 Then God said, "Let Us make man in Our image, according to Our likeness; and let them rule over the fish of the sea and over the birds of the sky and over the cattle and over all the earth, and over every creeping thing that creeps on the earth."

27 God created man in His own image, in the image of God He created him; male and female He created them.

28 God blessed them; and God said to them, "Be fruitful and multiply, and fill the earth, and subdue it; and rule over the fish of the sea and over the birds of the sky and over every living thing that moves on the earth."

GENESIS 2:18,21-25

18 Then the LORD God said, "It is not good for the man to be alone; I will make him a helper suitable for him."

21 So the LORD God caused a deep sleep to fall upon the man, and he slept; then He took one of his ribs and closed up the flesh at that place.

DISCUSS

• What was God's command to the man and woman in verse 28?

• Who created woman?

• How was she created?

• In what ways is her creation story similar to the man's? In what ways is it different?

• According to the verses you just read and marked, what do you see as the distinctive purpose of the woman?

• Discuss why knowing this truth is so important in today's society.

22 The LORD God fashioned into a woman the rib which He had taken from the man, and brought her to the man.

23 The man said, "This is now bone of my bones, and flesh of my flesh; she shall be called Woman, because she was taken out of Man."

24 For this reason a man shall leave his father and his mother, and be joined to his wife; and they shall become one flesh.

25 And the man and his wife were both naked and were not ashamed.

1 PETER 3:7

You husbands in the same way, live with your wives in an understanding way, as with someone weaker, since she is a woman; and show her honor as a fellow heir of the grace of life, so that your prayers will not be hindered.

GENESIS 3:16

To the woman He said, "I will greatly multiply your pain in childbirth, in pain you will bring forth children; yet your desire will be for your husband, and he will rule over you."

OBSERVE

Leader: *Read 1 Peter 3:7 aloud.*
- *Have the group circle every reference to **woman,** including synonyms and pronouns.*

DISCUSS

- What did you learn from marking the references to woman?

OBSERVE

When Adam and Eve ate from the tree of the knowledge of good and evil, their circumstances changed dramatically. Now they were sinners (Romans 5:12), and they no longer enjoyed an intimate relationship with God. Genesis 3:16 details the consequences of the woman's sin.

Leader: *Read Genesis 3:16 aloud. Have the group...*
- *circle every reference to **the woman,** including pronouns.*
- *draw a cloud like this* ☁ *around the word **desire.***

DISCUSS

• What were the consequences of the woman's disobedience?

INSIGHT

The Hebrew word translated here as *desire* is used only three times in the Bible. It appears in Genesis 3:16 and 4:7 and again in Song of Solomon 7:10. It means "to long for" or "to stretch out after." How a word or phrase is interpreted depends on the context in which it appears. Here the word *desire* is used in a context of sin and judgment. For this reason, many commentators believe that, because of sin, Eve would now desire to overtake Adam, to rule over him.

OBSERVE

Leader: *Read Genesis 4:7 aloud.*
   • *Have the group draw a cloud around the word **desire.***

GENESIS 4:7

If you do well, will not your countenance be lifted up? And if you do not do well, sin is crouching at the door; and its desire is for you, but you must master it.

DISCUSS

• In light of this passage, how would you explain the statement "your desire will be for your husband, and he will rule over you" in Genesis 3:16?

• Why do you think God said this after the Fall?

EPHESIANS 5:18-23,33

18 And do not get drunk with wine, for that is dissipation, but be filled with the Spirit,

19 speaking to one another in psalms and hymns and spiritual songs, singing and making melody with your heart to the Lord;

20 always giving thanks for all things in the name of our Lord

OBSERVE

Ephesians 5:18-33 is probably the most important passage in the Bible regarding the husband-wife relationship. We looked at several of these verses last week while examining the man's role in marriage; let's now see what Paul had to say regarding the woman's role.

Leader: *Read Ephesians 5:18-23,33 aloud. Have the group...*
- *circle every reference to **wives**, including pronouns.*
- *underline every reference to **husbands**, including pronouns and synonyms.*

INSIGHT

The Greek verb translated as *subject* in verse 21 is *hupotasso,* which means "to place under" or "to arrange under." It is in the present tense, meaning that this action is to be continual, as a habit of life.

DISCUSS

• What did you learn from these verses about the role of the woman in marriage? According to verses 22 and 33, what are the two things a wife is commanded to do?

• According to verse 22, submission to your husband is obedience to whom?

• According to what you have observed in this passage, should a man force his wife to submit? Explain your answer.

• Keeping in mind the context of this passage, discuss the intended meaning of Paul's instructions to the wife. Also, keep in mind what you learned last week about

Jesus Christ to God, even the Father;

21 and be subject to one another in the fear of Christ.

22 Wives, be subject to your own husbands, as to the Lord.

23 For the husband is the head of the wife, as Christ also is the head of the church, He Himself being the Savior of the body.

33 Nevertheless, each individual among you also is to love his own wife even as himself, and the wife must see to it that she respects her husband.

the man's role. Was he telling women to submit to abuse? Is a wife to be a doormat or a punching bag? Is she to lie, steal, cheat, or commit adultery if her husband tells her to do so?

• What are the limits, if any, to biblical submission of the wife to her husband? Explain your answer.

OBSERVE

Let's look at some of Paul's other statements regarding the marriage relationship to see if they help clarify what biblical submission looks like.

COLOSSIANS 3:18

Wives, be subject to your husbands, as is fitting in the Lord.

Leader: Read Colossians 3:18.
    • *Have the group circle* **wives.**

DISCUSS

• How does this parallel with what we just read in Ephesians 5:22-23?

OBSERVE

Leader: Read 1 Corinthians 11:3 aloud.

   • *Have the group circle* **woman** *and underline* **man** *as before.*

DISCUSS

• Once again, draw a simple diagram to illustrate the roles of headship and submission described in this passage.

• What is Christ's relationship to God the Father?

• John 10:30 records Jesus saying, "I and the Father are one." In light of this and other passages of Scripture, does 1 Corinthians 11:3 indicate that Christ is less important than, or inferior to, the Father in some way?

• What then does this passage reveal to you about the wife's role within the marriage relationship?

---

1 CORINTHIANS 11:3

But I want you to understand that Christ is the head of every man, and the man is the head of a woman, and God is the head of Christ.

TITUS 2:3-5

3 Older women likewise are to be reverent in their behavior, not malicious gossips nor enslaved to much wine, teaching what is good,

4 so that they may encourage the young women to love their husbands, to love their children,

5 to be sensible, pure, workers at home, kind, being subject to their own husbands, so that the word of God will not be dishonored.

OBSERVE

Leader: *Read Titus 2:3-5 aloud.*

- *Have the group circle every reference to* **women,** *including pronouns.*

DISCUSS

- What behavior does God expect of the married woman?

- What are her responsibilities?

PROVERBS 31:10-31

10 An excellent wife, who can find? For her worth is far above jewels.

11 The heart of her husband trusts in her, and he will have no lack of gain.

OBSERVE

Leader: *Read Proverbs 31:10-31 aloud.*

- *Have the group circle every reference to* **the excellent wife,** *including pronouns.*

DISCUSS

• Discuss what you learned from this passage concerning the role of the woman.

12 She does him good and not evil all the days of her life.

13 She looks for wool and flax and works with her hands in delight.

14 She is like merchant ships; she brings her food from afar.

15 She rises also while it is still night and gives food to her household and portions to her maidens.

16 She considers a field and buys it; from her earnings she plants a vineyard.

17 She girds herself with strength and makes her arms strong.

18 She senses that her gain is good; her lamp does not go out at night.

19 She stretches out her hands to the distaff, and her hands grasp the spindle.

20 She extends her hand to the poor, and she stretches out her hands to the needy.

21 She is not afraid of the snow for her household, for all her household are clothed with scarlet.

22 She makes coverings for herself; her clothing is fine linen and purple.

23 Her husband is known in the gates, when he sits among the elders of the land.

24 She makes linen garments and sells them, and supplies belts to the tradesmen.

25 Strength and dignity

• How might the qualities and activities attributed to the "excellent wife" of Proverbs 31 be exhibited in the life of a woman today?

are her clothing, and she smiles at the future.

26 She opens her mouth in wisdom, and the teaching of kindness is on her tongue.

27 She looks well to the ways of her household, and does not eat the bread of idleness.

28 Her children rise up and bless her; her husband also, and he praises her, saying:

29 "Many daughters have done nobly, but you excel them all."

30 Charm is deceitful and beauty is vain, but a woman who fears the LORD, she shall be praised.

31 Give her the product of her hands, and let her works praise her in the gates.

WRAP IT UP

Women were created by God, made in His image yet distinctively female. Woman was created from man for man and given a role highly valued by God. She is to be man's *completer*, not his *competitor*. Not only is the woman physically different from a man, she's not wired the same emotionally. For this reason and others, God has given wives a role that is different from their husbands' yet equally important.

If we want to build marriages that really work, we need to embrace the truth of our gender differences and all they imply. What a difference it would make in so many marriages if we submitted to God's design and order. If you want to have the best marriage possible, then you must honor His plan. If you fight it, you will be fighting God. The consequences of such rebellion are continuing dissatisfaction, dissension, and eventually disaster.

What a privilege women have to reflect to the world the character and work of Jesus Christ in their roles as wives. Wives, what can you do this week to offer your husband respect and to more effectively fulfill your role as his completer?

Communication falls at the top of nearly everyone's list of ongoing marriage concerns. Countless books have been written on the topic, and it's a frequent focus of afternoon talk shows. Yet despite all the "expert" advice on communication techniques, homes are disintegrating due to communication problems.

This week we are going to look at God's thoughts, instructions, and commands regarding how we are to communicate with one another.

As you work through this lesson, ask God to reveal to you the effect of your words on other people, especially your spouse and children. Ask Him to show you your strengths and to help you discover how to improve any areas of weakness or failure in your communication skills.

OBSERVE

Let's begin our study this week by looking at a passage of Scripture that deals with a member of our body that is difficult to tame despite its small size. James 3 focuses on the tongue, on how we speak to one another. The writer begins verse 2 with "for we all stumble in many ways"—a simple yet profound statement. If we could just remember this in our marriages: We all stumble—every one of us—yet God urges us on to perfection.

JAMES 3:1-8

¹ Let not many of you become teachers, my brethren, knowing that as such we will incur a stricter judgment.

² For we all stumble in many ways. If anyone does not stumble in what he says, he is a perfect man, able to bridle the whole body as well.

³ Now if we put the bits into the horses' mouths so that they will obey us, we direct their entire body as well.

⁴ Look at the ships also, though they are so great and are driven by strong winds, are still directed by a very small rudder wherever the inclination of the pilot desires.

Leader: Read aloud James 3:1-8.

• *Have the group draw a squiggly line like this ⌇⌇⌇⌇ under every reference to **the tongue** or **speaking,** including all pronouns and synonyms such as **what he says.***

DISCUSS

• What did you learn from marking the references to the tongue and speaking?

• What did you learn from verse 2 about the person who bridles his or her tongue?

• Discuss the two pictures James uses in verses 4-6 to illustrate the impact of the tongue despite its small size.

• Describe an occasion when someone you know was affected by another person's words, either negatively or positively.

• What does this passage reveal about how you should speak to your spouse? How important to your marriage are the words you say?

• Remember the childhood chant "Sticks and stones may break my bones, but words will never hurt me"? Is this true, according to these verses?

5 So also the tongue is a small part of the body, and yet it boasts of great things. See how great a forest is set aflame by such a small fire!

6 And the tongue is a fire, the very world of iniquity; the tongue is set among our members as that which defiles the entire body, and sets on fire the course of our life, and is set on fire by hell.

7 For every species of beasts and birds, of reptiles and creatures of the sea, is tamed and has been tamed by the human race.

8 But no one can tame the tongue; it is a restless evil and full of deadly poison.

JAMES 3:9-12

⁹ With it we bless our Lord and Father, and with it we curse men, who have been made in the likeness of God;

¹⁰ from the same mouth come both blessing and cursing. My brethren, these things ought not to be this way.

¹¹ Does a fountain send out from the same opening both fresh and bitter water?

¹² Can a fig tree, my brethren, produce olives, or a vine produce figs? Nor can salt water produce fresh.

OBSERVE

Leader: *Read James 3:9-12 aloud.*

- *Again, have the group draw a squiggly line under every reference to **the tongue** or **the mouth**, including the pronoun **it**.*

DISCUSS

- What contrasts are given in verses 9 and 10 in respect to the tongue and the mouth?

- What do the two illustrations in verses 11 and 12 reveal as the problem of the tongue?

- According to this passage, what do inappropriate words reveal about the condition of your heart?

OBSERVE

Jesus said that man speaks out of the abundance of his heart. You've heard it said that "what's down in the well comes up in the bucket." What is down in your well—sweet water that refreshes, or bitter water that brings sickness and destruction? The answer lies within our hearts.

Leader: Read Matthew 12:33-37 aloud. Have the group…

• *draw a squiggly line under every reference to* **speaking, the mouth,** *and* **words.**

• *mark the word* **heart** *like this:* ♡

DISCUSS

• What did you learn from marking the key words in this passage?

• How do Jesus' words relate to what you read in James 3?

• What influences the way we speak?

MATTHEW 12:33-37

33 "Either make the tree good and its fruit good, or make the tree bad and its fruit bad; for the tree is known by its fruit.

34 "You brood of vipers, how can you, being evil, speak what is good? For the mouth speaks out of that which fills the heart.

35 "The good man brings out of his good treasure what is good; and the evil man brings out of his evil treasure what is evil.

36 "But I tell you that every careless word that people speak, they shall give an accounting for it in the day of judgment.

37 "For by your words you will be justified, and by your words you will be condemned."

- What sort of power do our words carry? Explain your answer thoroughly; don't miss verses 36-37.

- Based on what you have just read, what is the key to communicating in a way that honors God and ministers to our spouses? How is this accomplished in our lives?

JAMES 1:26

If anyone thinks himself to be religious, and yet does not bridle his tongue but deceives his own heart, this man's religion is worthless.

OBSERVE

Leader: Read James 1:26 aloud. Have the group...

- *mark **tongue** with a squiggly line as before.*
- *draw a heart over the word **heart**.*

DISCUSS

- What is the connection between one's tongue and one's "religion," or profession of faith?

- What does your tongue reveal about your religion?

OBSERVE

Leader: *Read aloud the passages printed out for you on this and the following page—through Proverbs 18:21. Have the group...*

- *draw a squiggly line under every term like **mouth** and words that refer to **speaking.***
- *mark the word **heart** with a heart.*

DISCUSS

- Read each passage and discuss all that you learned. Give some practical examples of how these principles could be lived out in your marriage relationship.

- Which verse might your spouse use to describe your usual way of communicating?

JOB 16:5

I could strengthen you with my mouth, and the solace of my lips could lessen your pain.

PROVERBS 4:24

Put away from you a deceitful mouth and put devious speech far from you.

PROVERBS 11:11

By the blessing of the upright a city is exalted, but by the mouth of the wicked it is torn down.

PROVERBS 16:21,23-24

21 The wise in heart will be called understanding, and sweetness of speech increases persuasiveness.

23 The heart of the wise instructs his mouth and adds persuasiveness to his lips.

24 Pleasant words are a honeycomb, sweet to the soul and healing to the bones.

PROVERBS 17:27-28

27 He who restrains his words has knowledge, and he who has a cool spirit is a man of understanding.

28 Even a fool, when he keeps silent, is considered wise; when he closes his lips, he is considered prudent.

PROVERBS 18:21

21 Death and life are in the power of the tongue, and those who love it will eat its fruit.

INSIGHT

Remember the long hours you spent in conversation while dating? You looked forward to the phone's ring so you could hear those encouraging, complimentary words that were as sweet as honey to your ears.

How does this compare with your discussions with your spouse these days? Are your phone conversations short, curt, and to the point? Are your evenings spent in front of the television or computer rather than in long, exhilarating conversation? If so, you may wonder if you can ever return to the loving conversations of your early relationship. You can, but it will take work and a conscious effort. Healthy, meaningful communication doesn't just happen overnight, but it is possible.

OBSERVE

Every marriage relationship will include points of agreement and disagreement. Discussing your differences while practicing healthy communication is a fine art, especially when that tiny member of our body—the tongue—is so easily "set on the fire by hell" (James 1:6). God has laid out in His Word principles for handling disagreements without causing damage to your relationship.

Leader: Read aloud the passages printed out on this and the following pages—through James 1:19-20. Have the group mark the following:

- each reference to **speaking,** including **word, mouth,** and other synonyms, with a squiggly line.
- each occurrence of the word **heart** with a heart.
- each reference to **anger** by drawing a box around it.

PROVERBS 15:1

A gentle answer turns away wrath, but a harsh word stirs up anger.

PROVERBS 15:28

The heart of the righteous ponders how to answer, but the mouth of the wicked pours out evil things.

PROVERBS 18:13

He who gives an answer before he hears, it is folly and shame to him.

EPHESIANS 4:26

Be angry, and yet do not sin; do not let the sun go down on your anger.

EPHESIANS 4:29-31

29 Let no unwholesome word proceed from your mouth, but

only such a word as is good for edification according to the need of the moment, so that it will give grace to those who hear.

30 Do not grieve the Holy Spirit of God, by whom you were sealed for the day of redemption.

31 Let all bitterness and wrath and anger and clamor and slander be put away from you, along with all malice.

COLOSSIANS 4:6

Let your speech always be with grace, as though seasoned with salt, so that you will know how you should respond to each person.

DISCUSS

• Discuss one by one the principles God provided in these passages to help us communicate properly with our mates (and others), even when we disagree.

• Which of these instructions is the most difficult for you? Why?

JAMES 1:19-20

19 This you know, my beloved brethren. But everyone must be quick to hear, slow to speak and slow to anger;

20 for the anger of man does not achieve the righteousness of God.

WRAP IT UP

Carefully chosen words can change the course of a child's life, disarm the accuser, calm the storm, build up the downtrodden, and give hope to the hopeless. Just think what would happen in our marriages if husbands and wives would simply consider their words—before they speak! Healthy and clear communication is a vital component of a marriage relationship that brings honor and glory to God.

Ask the Lord to make you aware of things you've said to your spouse for which you need to ask forgiveness. Ask God to show you any problem within your heart that needs to be resolved, then deal thoroughly with what He reveals. If you have demeaned or offended with your words, confess your wrong to God and your spouse and begin immediately to change your style of communication.

Seek the opportunity this week to spend some time with your spouse and each member of your family, asking if you have said anything that has hurt them. If they share something, do not defend yourself. Simply agree that you were wrong and ask their forgiveness. Remember, whether or not it was your intent, they were wounded by your words. Don't be defensive.

Remember, "death and life are in the power of the tongue" (Proverbs 18:21). Your words have the power to give life to a relationship or kill it. Choose to be a man or woman who bridles the tongue, one whose religion is evident. Make a concentrated effort to build people up with your words. Try it for a week and watch what happens!

No term in our modern vocabulary has been more used, abused, perverted, or misunderstood than the simple four-letter word *love*. We might say "I love chocolate" with the same level of enthusiasm as "I love you."

We frequently hear of people who choose to divorce because one spouse or both have "fallen out of love." What happened? Can love really fade away? Is everlasting love an unattainable dream?

The answer depends on the kind of love your relationship was built on. You need to understand the kind of love that will never end. It is a matter of obedience rather than emotion. If you can grasp this truth and live in the light of it, you can build a marriage that will last "until death us do part."

OBSERVE

Love is one of the most-used words in the Bible. To really understand love, we must begin with God, because He is not only the source of love but also the One who designed us with a need to give and receive love.

Leader: *Read John 3:16 and 1 John 4:7-21 aloud. Have the group…*

- *mark each occurrence of **love** with a heart:* ♡
- *mark every reference to **God**, including pronouns, with a triangle:* △

JOHN 3:16

For God so loved the world, that He gave His only begotten Son, that whoever believes in Him shall not perish, but have eternal life.

1 JOHN 4:7-21

7 Beloved, let us love one another, for love is from God; and everyone

who loves is born of God and knows God.

8 The one who does not love does not know God, for God is love.

9 By this the love of God was manifested in us, that God has sent His only begotten Son into the world so that we might live through Him.

10 In this is love, not that we loved God, but that He loved us and sent His Son to be the propitiation for our sins.

11 Beloved, if God so loved us, we also ought to love one another.

12 No one has seen God at any time; if we love one another, God abides in us, and His love is perfected in us.

INSIGHT

Four Greek words are used for love. Once we grasp their meaning, it will be easier to understand why some people talk about "falling out of love."

Storge refers to natural affection or obligation. Its basis is one's own nature. *Storge* is that natural affection that wells up within for your spouse, your child, or even your dog. Because it is based on human nature, it can come and go. It is used in the New Testament only in the negative, as *astorge.*

Eros indicates a passion that seizes and overmasters the mind. It is an erotic love. This kind of love typifies our culture. It is a self-centered love that looks primarily for what it can receive. When it gives, it does so in order to receive. *Eros* is a conditional love. This Greek word for love is not found in the Bible.

Phileo is often described as brotherly love. It is the love of fond companionship, a sense of pleasure

(continued on page 63)

(continued from page 62)

in the presence of another. It differs from *eros* in that it wants to give as well as receive. *Phileo* responds to acts of kindness, tenderness, or appreciation. It is concerned about the other's happiness as well as its own.

Agape is love that takes the initiative in the relationship regardless of what response it might receive. John uses this term to describe God's love for a world that did not know Him (verse 10). In the New Testament *agape* became associated with selflessness, primarily because of the unconditional love the Father expressed when He gave His Son as a sacrifice for sin. When the Bible says "God is love," this is the kind of love He is. God's love gives and gives and gives, even when the loved one is unresponsive. The early church used this word to describe the kind of love that should distinguish believers from the world. If God so loved us, we also in the same way ought to love one another.

13 By this we know that we abide in Him and He in us, because He has given us of His Spirit.

14 We have seen and testify that the Father has sent the Son to be the Savior of the world.

15 Whoever confesses that Jesus is the Son of God, God abides in him, and he in God.

16 We have come to know and have believed the love which God has for us. God is love, and the one who abides in love abides in God, and God abides in him.

17 By this, love is perfected with us, so that we may have confidence in the day of

judgment; because as He is, so also are we in this world.

18 There is no fear in love; but perfect love casts out fear, because fear involves punishment, and the one who fears is not perfected in love.

19 We love, because He first loved us.

20 If someone says, "I love God," and hates his brother, he is a liar; for the one who does not love his brother whom he has seen, cannot love God whom he has not seen.

21 And this commandment we have from Him, that the one who loves God should love his brother also.

DISCUSS

The love spoken of in these passages is *agape*, as described in the Insight box. Keep this in mind as you answer the following questions:

• According to these passages, where does love originate?

• Is this type of love passive or active? Explain your answer.

• Discuss what you learned about love from these passages.

• Look again at the Insight box. Which kind of love are followers of Christ supposed to demonstrate?

• Discuss how what you just learned about love applies to the marriage relationship. For example, what if your husband or wife doesn't look the way he or she did when you first began to date? What if your mate doesn't talk to you like he or she did when you were dating?

• Why do you think we are not commanded to love with a *storge* or *eros* kind
of love? Is God against these? Explain
your answer.

OBSERVE

*Leader: Read aloud John 13:34; Ephesians
5:25; and Romans 13:8-10.*
  • *Have the group mark each reference to
  love with a heart, as before.*

DISCUSS

• Once again, the Greek word for *love* used
in these verses is *agape*. Discuss what you
learned about love from marking these
passages.

• What is the purest example of this kind of
love?

JOHN 13:34

[Jesus is speaking.]

A new commandment
I give to you, that you
love one another, even
as I have loved you,
that you also love one
another.

EPHESIANS 5:25

Husbands, love your
wives, just as Christ also
loved the church and
gave Himself up for her.

ROMANS 13:8-10

8 Owe nothing to
anyone except to love
one another; for he
who loves his neighbor
has fulfilled the law.

9 For this, "You shall not commit adultery, You shall not murder, You shall not steal, You shall not covet," and if there is any other commandment, it is summed up in this saying, "You shall love your neighbor as yourself."

10 Love does no wrong to a neighbor; therefore love is the fulfillment of the law.

1 CORINTHIANS 13:4-8,13

4 Love is patient, love is kind and is not jealous; love does not brag and is not arrogant,

5 does not act unbecomingly; it does not seek its own, is not provoked, does not take into account a wrong suffered,

• There is no command for wives to love their husbands. Does this mean wives are exempt from loving their husbands? Explain your answer.

OBSERVE

To better understand how this love—*agape*—operates on a deeper level, let's take a look at a portion of the well-known "love chapter."

Leader: *Read 1 Corinthians 13:4-8,13 aloud.*

• *Once again, have the group mark each reference to **love,** including pronouns, with a heart.*

DISCUSS

• Discuss the characteristics of love described in this passage and illustrate how each relates to the marriage relationship.

• What are some practical ways to show love to your spouse?

• If Christian husbands and wives began to love each other as described in 1 Corinthians 13, what impact would that have on families, churches, communities, and our nation?

• Can this type of love be demonstrated apart from God? Who then can love this way? Explain your answer.

• In light of all you have learned this week, when someone says he has "fallen out of love," what does he really mean? Where did his love go? Explain your answer.

6 does not rejoice in unrighteousness, but rejoices with the truth;

7 bears all things, believes all things, hopes all things, endures all things.

8 Love never fails; but if there are gifts of prophecy, they will be done away; if there are tongues, they will cease; if there is knowledge, it will be done away.

13 But now faith, hope, love, abide these three; but the greatest of these is love.

WRAP IT UP

We saw in this week's study that God's love is a love that initiates, that acts. It would have been impossible for God to say "I love you" and then withhold Jesus from us. Real love has to be expressed.

We love because He first loved us, and He expressed that love in a selfless, sacrificial way. God expects His followers to demonstrate a love that mirrors His.

If God intended for *agape* love to be displayed by believers to the whole world, He also meant for it to be at work in the marriage relationship. Now that you've learned God's standard on this subject, evaluate your love for your spouse. Is your relationship based on *agape* love—or on *eros* or *storge* love? Are your expressions of love selfless, sacrificial? If not, are you willing to make the changes necessary to love your spouse according to God's standard? What if your spouse doesn't respond to this love; can you stop loving him or her? Is this even possible?

Remember, the expression of *agape* is always a choice; its source is obedience rather than emotion. When your emotions turn toward anger or frustration, when the passion fades, when your love is not reciprocated, how will you respond? Will you choose to love as God instructs?

Marriage counselors tell us that money is the source of a great deal of marital strife. When a couple can't agree on how to handle their money, their disagreements will eventually spill over into other areas of their relationship. The pressures of financial difficulty can crush the life out of even a good marriage. Often such problems could be totally avoided by knowing and following God's instructions concerning finances. This week we will look at some principles that can protect us from money trouble or help us find a way out of it.

OBSERVE

A proper attitude and perspective about finances depends on your knowing and resting in God's promises concerning your needs. Let's see what Jesus had to say on this subject.

Leader: *Read Matthew 6:19-21,24-25,31-33 aloud. Have the group...*

- *draw a box around every reference to* **treasure** *and* **wealth,** *including synonyms.*
- *underline each* **instruction** *Jesus gave to His listeners.*

MATTHEW 6:19-21, 24-25,31-33

19 "Do not store up for yourselves treasures on earth, where moth and rust destroy, and where thieves break in and steal.

20 "But store up for yourselves treasures in heaven, where neither moth nor rust destroys, and where thieves do not break in or steal;

21 for where your treasure is, there your heart will be also.

24 "No one can serve two masters; for either he will hate the one and love the other, or he will be devoted to one and despise the other. You cannot serve God and wealth.

25 "For this reason I say to you, do not be worried about your life, as to what you will eat or what you will drink; nor for your body, as to what you will put on. Is not life more than food, and the body more than clothing?

31 "Do not worry then, saying, 'What will we eat?' or 'What will we drink?' or 'What will we wear for clothing?'

DISCUSS

• What did you learn concerning your finances by marking references to treasure and wealth in this passage?

• Discuss each of God's commands and how they apply to us today. What gives us the confidence to obey them?

• What does Jesus tell us we cannot do? Why not?

• What is the Father's promise to His children?

• What condition, if any, is attached to this promise?

• Where are you storing up treasure—on earth or in heaven? What does your answer reveal about your view of God?

32 "For the Gentiles eagerly seek all these things; for your heavenly Father knows that you need all these things.

33 "But seek first His kingdom and His righteousness, and all these things will be added to you."

• What action, if any, do you need to take?

OBSERVE

Jesus urged His followers to resist the fleshly inclination to accumulate things and instead trust God to provide for their needs. Let's look at some other passages that describe where we're to turn to have our needs met.

Leader: Read aloud Philippians 4:6-7,11-12,19; 1 Peter 5:6-7; and Psalm 37:25. Have the group…
  • *underline the instructions in each passage.*
  • *mark every reference to God, including pronouns, with a triangle:* △

PHILIPPIANS 4:6-7, 11-12,19

6 Be anxious for nothing, but in everything by prayer and supplication with thanksgiving let your requests be made known to God.

7 And the peace of God, which surpasses all comprehension, will guard your hearts and your minds in Christ Jesus.

11 Not that I speak from want, for I have learned to be content in whatever circumstances I am.

12 I know how to get along with humble means, and I also know how to live in prosperity; in any and every circumstance I have learned the secret of being filled and going hungry, both of having abundance and suffering need.

19 And my God will supply all your needs according to His riches in glory in Christ Jesus.

1 PETER 5:6-7

6 Therefore humble yourselves under the mighty hand of God, that He may exalt you at the proper time,

DISCUSS

• We all have basic material needs. How are these needs to be met?

• Does God care about your needs? From all you have read so far, explain your answer.

• What instructions are given to us in these passages? How do they relate to your finances?

• How might material wealth—or lack thereof—cause discontent or tension in marriage? What truths have you seen in these verses that might help you avoid or resolve any disagreements in this area?

OBSERVE

The book of Proverbs is a profound source of wisdom on many topics, including finances and giving.

Leader: Read aloud Proverbs 3:9-10; 22:1-2,7; 23:4-5; 28:27. Have the group…

• *draw a box around every reference to* **wealth,** *including pronouns and synonyms.*

• *draw a squiggly line under* **poor,** *like this:* ∽∽∽∽

7 casting all your anxiety on Him, because He cares for you.

PSALM 37:25

I have been young and now I am old, yet I have not seen the righteous forsaken or his descendants begging bread.

PROVERBS 3:9-10

9 Honor the LORD from your wealth and from the first of all your produce;

10 so your barns will be filled with plenty and your vats will overflow with new wine.

PROVERBS 22:1-2,7

1 A good name is to be more desired than great wealth, favor is better than silver and gold.

2 The rich and the poor have a common bond, the LORD is the maker of them all.

7 The rich rules over the poor, and the borrower becomes the lender's slave.

PROVERBS 23:4-5

4 Do not weary yourself to gain wealth, cease from your consideration of it.

5 When you set your eyes on it, it is gone. For wealth certainly makes itself wings like an eagle that flies toward the heavens.

PROVERBS 28:27

He who gives to the poor will never want, but he who shuts his eyes will have many curses.

DISCUSS

• Discuss what you learned about your personal finances from marking references to wealth.

• What should be your attitude toward attaining riches? Why?

• What is your responsibility to the poor?

• What principles are you to follow concerning borrowing and lending?

• Does your handling of money reflect the wisdom given in these verses? Are you honoring God with your wealth? What has been your attitude toward finances up to now? What, if anything, will you change because of what you've learned today?

OBSERVE

Our society places a great deal of emphasis on living well, getting all you can, attaining more, and becoming wealthy. Let's see how the world's view of success compares with God's Word.

Leader: *Read 1 Timothy 6:8-10,17-19 aloud. Have the group...*

- *draw a box around each reference to **money**, including pronouns and synonyms.*
- *underline each **instruction** given in this passage.*

DISCUSS

- What do these verses reveal about God's perspective on money and the pursuit of wealth?

- What did you learn from marking the instructions in this passage?

1 TIMOTHY 6:8-10,17-19

8 If we have food and covering, with these we shall be content.

9 But those who want to get rich fall into temptation and a snare and many foolish and harmful desires which plunge men into ruin and destruction.

10 For the love of money is a root of all sorts of evil, and some by longing for it have wandered away from the faith and pierced themselves with many griefs.

17 Instruct those who are rich in this present world not to be conceited or to fix their hope on the uncertainty of riches, but on

God, who richly supplies us with all things to enjoy.

18 Instruct them to do good, to be rich in good works, to be generous and ready to share,

19 storing up for themselves the treasure of a good foundation for the future, so that they may take hold of that which is life indeed.

ECCLESIASTES 5:10-20

10 He who loves money will not be satisfied with money, nor he who loves abundance with its income. This too is vanity.

11 When good things increase, those who consume them increase. So what

• What does the writer of this passage say about those who want to get rich? How does this differ from what he said about those who already are rich?

• In what ways does the world's financial "wisdom" correspond to or contradict the perspective on wealth offered in these verses?

OBSERVE

While concern over wealth and material possessions may seem to be a modern problem, the ancient book of Ecclesiastes, written by King Solomon—the wisest man who ever lived and also one of the wealthiest—reveals that mankind has always struggled in this area.

Leader: *Read Ecclesiastes 5:10-20 aloud.*

• *Have the group draw a box around every reference to* **money** *and* **riches,** *including synonyms and pronouns.*

DISCUSS

• King Solomon made a remarkable statement about people and money in verse 10. What did he say?

• Have you ever said you would be satisfied with a certain level of income, only to find that when you reach your goal you crave still more?

• What does verse 12 say is the difference between the working man and the rich man?

is the advantage to their owners except to look on?

12 The sleep of the working man is pleasant, whether he eats little or much; but the full stomach of the rich man does not allow him to sleep.

13 There is a grievous evil which I have seen under the sun: riches being hoarded by their owner to his hurt.

14 When those riches were lost through a bad investment and he had fathered a son, then there was nothing to support him.

15 As he had come naked from his mother's womb, so will he return as he came. He

will take nothing from the fruit of his labor that he can carry in his hand.

16 This also is a grievous evil—exactly as a man is born, thus will he die. So what is the advantage to him who toils for the wind?

17 Throughout his life he also eats in darkness with great vexation, sickness and anger.

18 Here is what I have seen to be good and fitting: to eat, to drink and enjoy oneself in all one's labor in which he toils under the sun during the few years of his life which God has given him; for this is his reward.

• What "grievous evil" is described in verses 13-15? Why is this a problem? Do these verses describe your "investment strategy"?

• What happened to the rich man's money? What practical truth does this illustrate regarding earthly wealth?

• Have you—or someone you've known— lost money in a bad business deal or in the stock market? Discuss the scenario.

• According to verse 15, of what value is the man's wealth at the end of his life?

• What is our responsibility in regard to money, according to verses 18-20? What will come as a result of a right attitude toward wealth and work?

• Have you been pursuing earthly treasures instead of God? If so, what are you going to do about it?

OBSERVE

Jesus said, "Then render to Caesar the things that are Caesar's; and to God the things that are God's" (Matthew 22:21). This verse is frequently quoted to affirm our obligation to pay taxes. However, we often overlook the point about giving to God what is due Him.

As we bring our study to a close, let's look at what God has to say about the practice of tithing, giving a portion of our income to the Lord.

Leader: *Read Leviticus 27:30-32 aloud.*
• *Have the group draw a box around each occurrence of* **tithe** *and* **tenth.**

19 Furthermore, as for every man to whom God has given riches and wealth, He has also empowered him to eat from them and to receive his reward and rejoice in his labor; this is the gift of God.

20 For he will not often consider the years of his life, because God keeps him occupied with the gladness of his heart.

LEVITICUS 27:30-32

30 Thus all the tithe of the land, of the seed of the land, or of the fruit of the tree, is the LORD's; it is holy to the LORD.

31 If, therefore, a man wishes to redeem part of his tithe, he shall add to it one-fifth of it.

32 For every tenth part of the herd or the flock, whatever passes under the rod, the tenth one shall be holy unto the LORD.

MALACHI 3:8-12

8 "Will a man rob God? Yet you are robbing Me! But you say, 'How have we robbed You?' In tithes and offerings.

9 "You are cursed with a curse, for you are robbing Me, the whole nation of you!

10 "Bring the whole tithe into the storehouse, so that there may be food in My house, and test Me now in this," says the LORD of hosts, "if I will not open for you the windows of

DISCUSS

• What principle did you learn from marking the key words in this passage?

OBSERVE

Leader: Read Malachi 3:8-12 aloud. Have the group…

> • *mark every reference to* **God,** *including* **Me, My,** *and* **Lord of hosts** *with a triangle.*
> • *draw a box around* **tithes** *and* **offerings.**

DISCUSS

• Briefly discuss what is happening in this passage.

• What did God tell the people to do in verse 10?

• What did God say He would do for them if they obeyed?

heaven and pour out for you a blessing until it overflows.

11 "Then I will rebuke the devourer for you, so that it will not destroy the fruits of the ground; nor will your vine in the field cast its grapes," says the LORD of hosts.

12 "All the nations will call you blessed, for you shall be a delightful land," says the LORD of hosts.

OBSERVE

The following passage was written by Paul to the believers in the city of Corinth, which was taking up a collection to help meet the needs of the believers elsewhere.

2 Corinthians 9:7-14

7 Each one must do just as he has purposed in his heart, not grudgingly or under compulsion, for God loves a cheerful giver.

8 And God is able to make all grace abound to you, so that always having all sufficiency in everything, you may have an abundance for every good deed;

9 as it is written, "He scattered abroad, he gave to the poor, His righteousness endures forever."

10 Now He who supplies seed to the sower and bread for food will supply and multiply your seed for sowing and increase the harvest of your righteousness;

Leader: *Read 2 Corinthians 9:7-14. Have the group...*

- *draw a box around every reference to **giving,** including words like **ministry** and **liberality.***
- *mark every reference to **God the Father** and **Jesus, the Son of God** with a triangle.*

DISCUSS

- From the references you marked, what did you observe about God in respect to our giving?

- What did you learn from these verses about the importance of the heart of the giver?

- According to this passage, what are the consequences of bountiful, or generous, giving? Make sure you cover the text carefully, as you don't want to miss a thing.

• Do you think most people today see giving as a ministry, a joy? Do we tend to recognize giving as something that brings glory to God because of the thanksgiving it produces? Explain your answers.

• According to verse 13, what is the connection between giving and one's confession, or belief, in the gospel of Christ?

• What is the most significant truth you learned this week? How are you going to apply it to your life?

• From all you have looked at this week regarding money, where do you stand? Have you looked to material wealth rather than to God for your security? Are you storing up for yourself treasures and robbing God? What is God's instruction?

11 you will be enriched in everything for all liberality, which through us is producing thanksgiving to God.

12 For the ministry of this service is not only fully supplying the needs of the saints, but is also overflowing through many thanksgivings to God.

13 Because of the proof given by this ministry, they will glorify God for your obedience to your confession of the gospel of Christ and for the liberality of your contribution to them and to all,

14 while they also, by prayer on your behalf, yearn for you because of the surpassing grace of God in you.

WRAP IT UP

It is simply amazing how much the Bible has to say about money. God knows that the need for money is a reality of our daily life, but He doesn't want us to worry about it. He calls us to "seek first His kingdom and His righteousness" (Matthew 6:33). When we do so, He promises to take care of us.

Do you give generously to others and to your church, trusting God to meet your needs? Or do you give grudgingly? Does your checkbook reflect the priority of God or self?

What does your heart seek? Are you building up treasures in heaven or on earth? Are you content with what you have? Or are you chasing after more, in effect telling God that you're not satisfied with His provision? God knows all your needs—every one—and He can meet those needs out of His abundance. He has already secured your future in heaven. Why not allow Him to take care of you now?

If you and your spouse allow God's financial principles to guide your decisions, you will eliminate many of the stresses married couples face. Your chances of harmony will increase and blessings will follow. Why not put God's financial wisdom to work in your marriage today? What do you have to lose?

FOR FURTHER READING

A Marriage Without Regrets by Kay Arthur. Eugene, OR:
Harvest House, 2000.

Money and Possessions: The Quest for Contentment by Kay
Arthur. Colorado Springs: WaterBrook Press, 2004.

This unique Bible study series from Kay Arthur and the teaching team of Precept Ministries International tackles the issues with which inquiring minds wrestle—in short, easy-to-grasp lessons ideal for small-group settings. The study courses in the series can be followed in any order. Here is one possible sequence:

How Do You Know God's Your Father?
by Kay Arthur, David and BJ Lawson

So many say "I'm a Christian," but how can they really know God's their Father—and that heaven's home? The short book of 1 John was written for that purpose—that you might *know* that you really do have eternal life. This is a powerful, enlightening study that will take you out of the dark and open your understanding to this key biblical truth.

Having a Real Relationship with God
by Kay Arthur

For those who yearn to know God and relate to Him in meaningful ways, Kay Arthur opens the Bible to show the way to salvation. With a straightforward examination of vital Bible passages, this enlightening study focuses on where we stand with God, how our sin keeps us from knowing Him, and how Christ bridged the chasm between humans and their Lord.

Being a Disciple: Counting the Real Cost
by Kay Arthur, Tom and Jane Hart

Jesus calls His followers to be disciples. And discipleship comes with a cost, a commitment. This study takes an inductive look at how the

Bible describes a disciple, sets forth the marks of a follower of Christ, and invites students to accept the challenge and then enjoy the blessings of discipleship.

How Do You Walk the Walk You Talk?

by Kay Arthur

This thorough, inductive study of Ephesians 4 and 5 is designed to help students see for themselves what God says about the lifestyle of a true believer in Jesus Christ. The study will equip them to live in a manner worthy of their calling, with the ultimate goal of developing a daily walk with God marked by maturity, Christlikeness, and peace.

Living a Life of True Worship

by Kay Arthur, Bob and Diane Vereen

Worship is one of Christianity's most misunderstood topics. This study explores what the Bible says about worship—what it is, when it happens, where it takes place. Is it based on your emotions? Is it something that only happens on Sunday in church? Does it impact how you serve? This study offers fresh, biblical answers.

Discovering What the Future Holds

by Kay Arthur, Georg Huber

With all that's transpiring in the world, people cannot help but wonder what the future holds. Will there ever be peace on earth? How long will the world live under the threat of terrorism? Is a one-world ruler on the horizon? This easy-to-use study guide leads readers through the book of Daniel, which sets forth God's blueprints for the future.

How to Make Choices You Won't Regret

by Kay Arthur, David and BJ Lawson

Every day we face innumerable decisions, some of which have the potential to change the course of our lives forever. Where do we go for direction? What do we do when faced with temptation? This fast-moving study offers practical, trustworthy guidelines by exploring the role of Scripture and the Holy Spirit in the decision-making process.

Money and Possessions: The Quest for Contentment

by Kay Arthur, David Arthur

Our attitudes toward money and possessions reflect the quality of our relationship with God. And, according to the Scriptures, our view of money reveals where our true affections lie. In this study readers dig into the Scriptures to learn where money comes from, how we're supposed to handle it, and how to live an abundant life, regardless of our financial circumstances.

How Can a Man Control His Thoughts, Desires, and Passions?

by Bob Vereen

This study equips men with the truth that God has provided everything we need to resist temptation. Through the examples of men in Scripture—those who fell into sin and those who stood firm—readers will find hope for controlling their passions, learn how to choose the path of purity, and find assurance that through the power of the Holy Spirit and God's Word, they can stand before God blameless and pure.

Living Victoriously in Difficult Times
by Kay Arthur, Bob and Diane Vereen

We live in a fallen world filled with fallen people, and we cannot escape hardship and pain. Somehow difficult times are a part of God's plan and they serve His purposes. This study helps readers discover how to glorify God in the midst of their pain. They'll learn how to find joy even when life seems unfair and experience the peace that comes from trusting in the One whose strength is made perfect in their weaknesses.

ABOUT THE AUTHORS

KAY ARTHUR, executive vice president and cofounder of Precept Ministries International, is known around the world as a Bible teacher, author, conference speaker, and host of the national radio and television programs *Precepts for Life.*

Kay and her husband, Jack, founded Precept Ministries in 1970 in Chattanooga, Tennessee. Started as a fledgling ministry for teens, Precept today is a worldwide outreach that establishes children, teens, and adults in God's Word, so that they can discover the Bible's truths for themselves. Precept inductive Bible studies are taught in all 50 states. The studies have been translated into 67 languages, reaching 120 countries.

DAVID AND BJ LAWSON serve as directors of the student ministry of Precept Ministries International. Both have been involved in Precept Ministries since the early 1980s and became staff members in 1997. David, a former police officer and pastor in Atlanta, is a coauthor with Kay Arthur and others of the International Inductive Study Series and a teacher on the Precept Upon Precept videos. BJ is a speaker and teacher for conferences and seminars. Both serve as trainers, working throughout the United States.